METHODIST CHURCHMANSHIP
AND ITS IMPLICATIONS

METHODIST CHURCHMANSHIP
AND ITS IMPLICATIONS

By

H. WATKIN-JONES
M.A., D.D.(Cantab.)

*Banks-Crossfield Tutor in Church History
and the History of Doctrine, Wesley College,
Headingley, Leeds*

δωρεὰν ἐλάβετε, δωρεὰν δότε.——MATTHEW x. 8.

THE EPWORTH PRESS
(EDGAR C. BARTON)
25 – 35 City Road, London, E.C.1

First published, 1946

TO

THE CHURCH OF MY FATHERS

Made in Great Britain

PREFACE

THE following chapters are an expansion of an article entitled 'Implications of Methodist Churchmanship' which appeared in the *Methodist Recorder* in November, 1943, and I acknowledge with gratitude the permission of the Editor to use that article as my foundation. I also express my thanks to Messrs. Charles Scribner's Sons, Ltd., publishers of *Church Music in History and Practice*, by Dr. Winfred Douglas, for permission to compose a footnote out of three pages of his book in the course of my chapter on 'Worship'. I have given full references to the publications to which I have alluded, in the event of a desire to read further concerning any part of the subject. It is my hope that this little book may help in answering questions about some of the things for which the Methodist Church stands. For what Methodist churchmanship is here held to imply, I must bear my own share of responsibility.

H. W.-J.

February, 1946.

CONTENTS

Christ loved the Church, and gave Himself up for it; that He might sanctify it, having cleansed it by the washing of water with the word, that He might present the Church to Himself a glorious Church, not having spot or wrinkle or any such thing; but that it should be holy and without blemish.

CHAPTER I

CHURCH OR SECT?

WHEN in 1932 the principal Methodist Communions became united they took occasion in their *Deed of Union* to assert together their full Churchmanship:

'The Methodist Church claims and cherishes its place in the Holy Catholic Church which is the Body of Christ.'

Five years later the Methodist Church declared:

'The true continuity with the Church of past ages which we cherish is to be found in the continuity of the Christian experience, the fellowship in the gift of the one Spirit; in the continuity of the allegiance to one Lord, the continued proclamation of the message, the continued acceptance of the mission.'[1] 'The Methodist Church . . . possesses those marks whereby, since the days of the Apostles, the Church has been known of men. Such are: the possession and acknowledgement of the Word of God as given in Scripture, and as interpreted by the Holy Spirit to the Church and to the individual; the profession of faith in God as He is incarnate and revealed in Christ; the observance of the Sacraments of Baptism and the Lord's Supper; and a ministry for the pastoral office, the preaching of the Word and the administration of the Sacraments.'[2]

It is for Methodism, therefore, to realize and to emphasize that she is a 'Church'—in the modern sense of that term. Methodists may need occasionally to defend this statement against criticism from outside their own communion; within it no shadow of doubt exists as to its truth.

[1] *The Nature of the Christian Church according to the teaching of the Methodists: Statement Approved by the Methodist Conference, Bradford, July, 1937*, p. 30.
[2] *ibid.*, p. 39.

It is the importance of what this truth implies which may now be worthy of attention; indeed, its implications are such that they strongly demand it.

It was highly significant that, within a few days of the close of the Uniting Conference of the Methodist Church, the editorial of the leading Methodist journal declared that 'one of the most important questions which Methodism has to face now is whether she is going to behave as a sect or as a branch of the Holy Catholic Church'.[1] Now much can be said in defence of sects and the sect outlook. In the Middle Ages it was a type which was 'a logical result of the Gospel', one which insistently appealed to the example of Christ and stressed personal inward holiness. Concerning it the historian, Troeltsch, observes: 'The sect does not live on the miracles of the past, nor on the miraculous nature of the institution, but on the constantly renewed miracle of the Presence of Christ, and on the subjective reality of the individual mastery of life.'[2] This insistence on personal devotion to Christ is actually and essentially Methodist. But the peril of the sect outlook is what Troeltsch calls 'a one-sided emphasis'—the cultivation of one expression of the Christian life, to the neglect of various doctrines (often the doctrine of the Church itself) which are not congenial to such an expression. Moreover, in Troeltsch's words, while the Church 'desires to cover the whole life of humanity', the sects 'aspire after personal inward perfection', and, so far from seeking to dominate the world, they are content to oppose it.[3] On the other hand—to quote from the same Methodist journal—'a Church stands for the whole truth of God, and welcomes into its fellowship lovers of Christ of every type. Moreover, a Church

[1] *The Methodist Recorder* 6th October, 1932.

[2] *The Social Teaching of the Christian Churches*, by Ernst Troeltsch (E. tr.), Vol. I, p. 341 (George Allen and Unwin).

[3] *ibid.*, p. 331.

aims not merely at adding individuals to its fellowship, but at extending the influence of the Christian religion among all secular institutions.'

While, then, Methodism has all along stood for a certain emphasis of the evangelical faith most precious to herself, and has made, and is still making, a valued contribution to the life and thought of the whole Church of Christ, she needs to bear in mind the perils of the sect outlook. 'It is most important that reunited Methodism should realize that she is called to be a branch of the Holy Catholic Church. This means that the whole truth of God must be proclaimed by her, that every lover of Christ, however different from the generally accepted Methodist type, must be able to find in her a congenial spiritual home, and that her members must widen their horizon and set out to permeate the secular world with the spirit of Jesus.'[1] This feature of Catholicity, or of the Universal nature and mission of the Church, is that which will be especially in our mind as we submit some considerations implied by Methodist Church-manship.

[1] *The Methodist Recorder, ibid.*

CHAPTER II

DOCTRINE

METHODIST doctrine is *Catholic* in the full sense, as having been received through the thought and experience of the centuries from the Primitive Church. Our Church, so the *Deed of Union* declares, 'rejoices in the inheritance of the Apostolic Faith and loyally accepts the fundamental principles of the historic creeds'. Belief in God as our Father, reconciling the world to Himself in the Person of His Divine and human Son, and active in the hearts of men by the power of His Holy Spirit: belief in the atoning death and resurrection of Christ, the Church which is His Body, the forgiveness of sins, and the life everlasting—such have been 'fundamental' in Methodist theology, in common with that of the ancient orthodox Communions of Christendom. We speak of 'fundamental principles' in that liberty of interpretation is allowed to the modern mind, which cannot be tied to antique philosophical ideas; but this refers in no sense to the facts of the Faith but only to their presentation. The truths relating to the Blessed Trinity and to Christ as Saviour have alone been the basis of the evangelical teaching and preaching of Methodism.

> *Te Deum laudamus. . . .*
> *Te per orbem terrarum sancta confitetur ecclesia,*
> *Patrem immensae maiestatis,*
> *Venerandum tuum verum et unicum Filium,*
> *Sanctum quoque Paracletum Spiritum.*

Next, Methodist doctrine is *Protestant*. 'The fundamental principles of the Protestant Reformation' are loyally accepted. So the *Deed of Union* proceeds: 'The Doctrines of the Evangelical Faith which Methodism has held from the beginning and still holds are based upon the Divine revelation recorded in the Holy Scriptures. The Methodist Church acknowledges this revelation as the supreme rule of faith and practice.' Accordingly, she proclaims the great Reformation doctrines of Salvation by faith only and the priesthood of all believers. As to the former, this was beyond doubt the belief of both Luther and Calvin,[1] and Wesley came to embrace it with all his heart.[2] He affirmed that his doctrine of justification by faith was the same as Calvin's, whose emphasis was on the supremacy of God's grace in salvation.[3] As to the latter doctrine, 'the Methodist Church,' so states the *Deed of Union*, 'holds the doctrine of the priesthood of all believers and consequently believes that no priesthood exists which belongs exclusively to a particular order or class of men, but in the exercise of its corporate life and worship special qualifications for the discharge of special duties are required and thus the principle of representative selection is recognized.' This was the Lutheran doctrine based on justification by *faith*. Its implication was that 'the God who had manifested Himself in Christ was accessible to every believing man'.[4] Each believer is a sacrificing priest—in a fellowship of Christian sacrifice.

[1] 'Nor will Calvin admit the possibility of justification by a mixture of faith and works. Some accept the idea of justification by faith, but object to that of faith alone. But, argues the Reformer, the one necessarily overthrows the other. Everyone who would obtain the righteousness of Christ must renounce his own so that every ground of boasting is excluded and man's salvation rests entirely on God's mercy.'—*Calvinism*, by A. Dakin, B.D., D.Theol., p. 77 (Duckworth).

[2] 'The immediate, essential, necessary means of reuniting men to God is living faith, and that alone. Without this, I cannot be reunited to God; with this, I cannot but be reunited.' Wesley, quoted by Dr. Henry Bett, *The Spirit of Methodism* (Epworth Press), p. 120.

[3] *The Rediscovery of John Wesley*, by George Croft Cell, p. 257 (Holt, New York).

[4] *The Nature of the Christian Church*, etc., p. 33.

Methodist doctrine is also *distinctive*. While holding tenaciously to all that has so far been mentioned, it has emphasized certain truths of evangelical experience: that all men may be saved through repentance and a personal reliance on Christ, that all may, by the power of the Holy Spirit, again through faith, attain to the holy life or 'perfect love to God and to man', and that the exultant assurance of personal acceptance with God may be the privilege of all believers in Christ. 'Wesley', writes Dr. Bett, 'never wavered from the belief that an experience of assurance is the normal result of a real penitence, a real faith, and a real surrender to Christ—that it is the privilege, and that it ought to be the possession of every redeemed soul.'[1] The stress was laid on the holy life as being utterly dependent on the grace of God.[2] Such doctrine is a complete refutation of humanism in the modern sense of the term; indeed, Wesley's early reactions in the pilgrimage of his spirit were against the leanings toward humanism found in Arminianism. It is emphatic on the absolute necessity of Divine Grace, and this very emphasis has always been characteristic of the Universal Church—certainly no less so now than at any period of her history.[3]

'Methodism', in the words of Dr. Scott Lidgett, 'is not sectarian, but evangelically catholic in its essential spirit.' While making its own contribution to the thought of the whole Church of Christ, it stands, even by reason of so doing, for the whole truth of the Gospel. Such is the attitude of a 'Church' as contrasted with that of a sect. But

---

[1] *The Spirit of Methodism*, p. 140. N.B. Wesley's tests of this: Scripture, fruits, and the correctives of fellowship.

[2] 'The Wesleyan reconstruction of the Christian ethic of life is an original and unique synthesis of the Protestant ethic of grace with the Catholic ethic of holiness.' Cell, *ibid.*, p. 347. Cf. my *Holy Spirit from Arminius to Wesley*, pp. 297 ff.

[3] 'There is in connexion with this subject [grace] no ground for maintaining division between the Churches.' *Report on the Edinburgh Conference on Faith and Order*, 1937.

modern Methodism needs not only to guard against the sect outlook, but also to beware of the slightest neglect of the supremacy of the grace of God operative through the Holy Spirit in the name of Christ. Nothing short of this will do for one moment, particularly in this present age, when the world's need of the Divine resources has been so tragically demonstrated. The searching question as to how far and how insistently we are proclaiming the full Gospel of the Divine Redeemer, in season and out of season, is indeed a test of the true exercise of our Churchmanship. Does such a test to any degree find us wanting? Do we sufficiently proclaim the fundamentals of the Christian Faith? If not, how far is this due to a feeling that 'doctrinal' sermons must almost inevitably be dull—when, rather, nothing could be more vitally preached than the immortal truths which should have seized the whole life of the preacher? Here, at least, is Wesley's testimony: 'From 1738 to this time, speaking continually of Jesus Christ, laying Him only for the foundation of the whole building, making Him all in all, the first and the last; preaching only on this plan, "The kingdom of God is at hand; repent ye and believe the Gospel"; the "word of God ran" as fire among the stubble.'[1] This is a reminder of our spiritual mission by which salvation, for both individual and society, can only rightly be proclaimed on the basis of the revelation of God in our Lord and Saviour Jesus Christ. 'I shrank not from declaring unto you the whole counsel of God' (Acts xx. 27). To shrink from that is to betray our Churchmanship.[2]

[1] Wesley's *Works*, VIII, p. 468. This and other similar passages are quoted in the booklet, *The Conversion of John Wesley*, by Richard Green, pp. 37 f. (F. Griffiths, 1909).

[2] It may be added that Methodist doctrine is not enforced in the sense of there being only one unalterable series of interpretations officially sanctioned. Thus the *Deed of Union*: 'Wesley's Notes on the New Testament and the first four volumes of his sermons . . . are not intended to impose a system of formal or speculative theology on Methodist Preachers but to set up standards

Continuation of footnote

of preaching and belief which should secure loyalty to the fundamental truths of the Gospel of Redemption and ensure the continued witness of the Church to the realities of the Christian experience of salvation.' Further, while the Conference cannot alter the doctrinal clauses of the Deed, it 'shall be the final authority within the Methodist Church with regard to all questions concerning the interpretation of its doctrines'. As far as legal language allows, here is encouragement to a forward look, to spiritual enterprise in theological thought, for which there is ever-increasing need.

CHAPTER III

THE SACRAMENTS

'THE Methodist Church recognizes two Sacraments, namely Baptism and the Lord's Supper, as of Divine appointment and of perpetual obligation, of which it is the privilege and duty of Members of the Methodist Church to avail themselves.' So again declares the *Deed of Union*. The Sacraments, together with the Word, are gifts of God to the Church for the salvation of men. They are channels for the operation of the Holy Spirit, whose gifts may be appropriated by faith; though 'the loving-kindness of God is not conceived as limited by His Sacraments'.[1] 'The presence of Christ through His Spirit in the Sacraments is realized by the faith of His people.'[2] As we are part of the Church of Christ, which in practically all of its branches has observed Baptism and the Lord's Supper throughout its history, we ought surely to maintain the position of importance which was given to the Sacraments by the earliest generations of Methodists.

As to Baptism, the significance of this received emphasis in the *Memorandum on Infant Baptism* which was accepted by the Conference in 1936, even as its importance had been stressed in the Standing Orders set up in 1932 as well as in the *Deed of Union*. The Methodist Church has never held that Baptism is essential to salvation, or that all who have been baptized are thereby saved.[3] Nevertheless, as is asserted in the *Memorandum*, 'in common with the general body of the Church of Christ', 'a solemn obligation to Christ, the Church, and the child rests upon parents to present their children to Christ in Baptism, and thus to honour the

[1] Edinburgh Conference on Faith and Order, 1937.
[2] Statement of the Wesleyan Methodist Conference, 1908.
[3] *The Holy Spirit from Arminius to Wesley*, pp. 248 ff.

ancient ordinance whereby they are joined to the visible community of Christ's people'.[1] Again, in the Report of the Methodist delegates to the World Conference on Faith and Order, 1937, the following statements occur:

'It was agreed that:

'1. "The sacraments are given by Christ to the Church as outward and visible signs of His invisible grace. They are not bare symbols, but pledges and seals of grace, and means whereby it is received."

'2. "Grace is bestowed in the sacraments within the fellowship of the Church by the personal action of Christ upon the believer. Faith is therefore a necessary condition for the reception of grace. . . ."

' "It is generally agreed that the united Church will observe the rule that all members of the visible Church are admitted by Baptism", and therefore "that Baptism in the name of the Trinity is the necessary bond of unity of the Christian Church". Most Christian Churches recognize and value the rule of infant Baptism.'

This neither upholds what is ordinarily understood as a doctrine of baptismal regeneration, nor does it mean that an unbaptized person is necessarily excluded from the Church. At the same time, Methodists must have their attitude to Baptism clarified, perhaps more than it is at present, particularly with regard to the sacramental nature of the rite and its relationship to communicant membership of the Church.[2]

[1] Without instruction in the home and the Church, Baptism may prove little more than a superstition, and in that event the advisability of its administration should be gravely considered. The Order of Service for the Baptism of Infants contains direct questions concerning both these circumstances.

[2] The Connexional Church Membership Committee, in its report to Conference in 1945, observed: 'The Committee finds itself facing fundamental questions about the meaning of Baptism, the nature of adult Church membership, and the contrast between the "natural" and "contractual" conceptions of the Church'; and rightly referred to these as 'theological issues'.

The Supper of the Lord, again, is in Methodist doctrine, not only a memorial, but a means of grace, used as such by the Holy Spirit wherever a living faith responds; it is a 'feeding on Christ in the heart by faith, with thanksgiving'. In John Wesley's sermon on *The Means of Grace* we read:

'All who desire an increase of the grace of God are to wait for it in partaking of the Lord's Supper: for this also is a direction Himself hath given. . . . And that this is also an ordinary, stated means of receiving the grace of God, is evident from those words of the Apostle . . . (1 Corinthians x. 16). Is not the eating of that bread, and the drinking of that cup, the outward visible means whereby God conveys into our souls all that spiritual grace, that righteousness, and peace, and joy in the Holy Ghost, which were purchased by the body of Christ once broken, and the blood of Christ once shed for us? Let all, therefore, who truly desire the grace of God, eat of that bread, and drink of that cup.'

It may be profitable in this connexion to remember the *Meditations on the Lord's Supper* which Wesley extracted from the writings of Thomas à Kempis, also *Hymns on the Lord's Supper* by Charles and himself, 'with a Preface concerning the Christian Sacrament and Sacrifice, extracted from Dr. Brevint', 'and sold at the New Chapel, City Road; and at the Rev. Mr. Wesley's Preaching-Houses, in Town and Country'. We may also remember Wesley's sermon on *The Duty of Constant Communion*, and the practice which he made of this, together with the fact that frequent Sacramental Services, both as confirming and converting ordinances, became a characteristic of the whole Methodist movement in the eighteenth century. The uncertainty of the four years immediately following Wesley's death regarding the administration of the Lord's Supper within the Methodist Societies, along with a meticulous regard for the Established Church, caused a break in the wonderful sacramental revival within Methodism, and it may be that we have never quite recovered from it.[1]

If this be so, ought we not to determine to recover from it? Our Church declares that the observance of this Sacrament is an obligation of our Churchmanship; and there is a further obligation, as the Standing Orders indicate, resting on our members to attend this ordinance as often as they are able. In no place, therefore, should the due observance of the Supper of the Lord be omitted, however small and remote the Methodist Society might be. For at the Lord's Table His presence by His Spirit is most preciously symbolized and as preciously realized by faith. Moreover 'the Eucharist is the supreme symbol of the fellowship of the Church. . . . It is primarily meant for the Christian community, and for the Christian individual.'[2] And for all Christians who believe that our Lord's command, 'Do this in remembrance of Me', is directed to members of His Church in all generations, 'can the neglect of' this Sacrament 'be called anything less than sin'?[3]

Within the Methodist family there have been somewhat varying traditions as to the form of service used at this Sacrament, and it may be that certain individual Churches would deem it wise not to be confined to one form

---

[1] 'Those four years of prohibition, followed by the restrictions of 1795, created a tradition which went far to annul the teaching and example of John Wesley, and sowed seeds of which we reap the harvest even to this day.' Art, 'The Place of the Lord's Supper in Early Methodism', by Thomas H. Barratt, B.A., in the London Quarterly Review, July, 1923. The whole article is most illuminating.

[2] The Sacramental Society (Fernley Lecture, 1927), by C. Ryder Smith, D.D., p. 181. A well-known view of the late Archbishop Temple is stated in his Introduction to Doctrine in the Church of England, being the Report of the Commission on Christian Doctrine appointed by the Archbishops of Canterbury and York in 1922: 'Christ is the Priest as well as the Victim; and in the Eucharist He unites us to Himself in His self-offering to the Father, as we feed upon Him in our hearts that He, who came to do God's will, may become the very life of our souls', p. 15 (S.P.C.K.).

[3] C. Ryder Smith, ibid., p. 177. It may be that more of our sick and infirm members would be grateful for a Sacramental Service in their homes if the offer were made to them.

alone—if so be that the presence of the crucified and risen Saviour is always reverently and lovingly realized. Yet the suggestion may perhaps be permitted that the more familiar form which appears in our Book of Offices has a threefold appeal. First, there is its appeal of antiquity—for those to whom such an appeal may be of value. It has been subjected to revisions since it substantially appeared as now in the second Prayer Book of Edward VI, yet parts of it go back to the times of the Primitive Christian Church, and it may prove helpful to remember that we still use sentences hallowed and proved precious through centuries of Christian worship. Second, it is a service in which all the communicants can take responsive part. Third, its range of thought is complete and satisfying, proceeding through the prayer for cleansing, the Divine Commandments or Beatitudes, the appropriate Collect, Epistle, and Gospel, the ancient Form of Christian belief, the prayer for the Church Militant with its sense of union with the Church Triumphant. From that point the service becomes still more intimate, moving through self-examination and confession to the prayer for pardon, the Comfortable Words, the prayers of Humble Access and of Institution: following the reception of the elements there come the act of personal dedication, the ancient Gloria, and the Blessing. All is here: except for an address where no sermon has preceded, one can think of no omission. Indeed, even without any address, the service is complete in itself. We may admit that Methodists often find the use of the full service extremely difficult; yet it has often been found an aid to that end to take the earlier part of the Communion Service in the more public part of the worship preceding it, while there is now a more frequent observance of this Sacrament as a service in itself. What is *supremely* important is the obligatory nature of the Supper of the Lord, and the duty which rests upon us all to make it regularly available for every Methodist.

CHAPTER IV

THE FELLOWSHIP OF THE CHURCH

(1) In Methodism this has always been a precious feature. It has been specifically a contribution on our part to the life and thought of the Universal Church. The brotherhood of the Ministry has been a rich reality to those who have been admitted to it, while it is common knowledge that spiritual fellowship, as expressed particularly by the 'Class-Meeting', has been woven into our very existence from the first. Whatever stress has been laid by Methodism upon individual conversion, it was never at the cost of a vital relation of the individual to the Society. Is this relation as vital now as it used to be? Who dare contend that it is?

Admittedly, there are several valuable groups in our local Churches, and in many of these groups the spiritual aim is obvious. But the 'Class-Meeting', once so great and so central a means of grace, has, to a large extent, suffered eclipse, though, in its essence, it appears here and there to be reviving. If our spiritual fellowship becomes, according to our own standards, increasingly defective, how can any spiritual 'forward movement' be expected to arise out of it? While an aggressive wing is gaining ground, the army threatens to cave in at the centre. The distressing shrinkage in the number of Methodist Church members since 1932 points alarmingly to this very fact. And Methodism, as a branch of the Church of Christ on earth, dare not ignore it. The Conference has declared that our members 'shall give assurance that they seek fellowship with Christ Himself and His people by taking up the duties and privileges of the Methodist Church', and that 'the Leaders' Meeting shall be satisfied of the sincerity of this desire, as shown by the evidence of life and conduct, and by fidelity to the ordinances of the Church and the maintenance of Christian ellowship and the means of grace'. Yet 'we find in many ases that membership has become haphazard and almost meaningless, instead of being a realized fellowship in the Body of Christ, calling for consecration and service, and etting an example of true community before the world'.[1] ometimes persons are members who ought not so to be, or who do not even know that they are members; on the other hand, are there not very many loyal Methodists who are in regular fellowship with us in worship and service who are not in actual Church membership at all? And in how many of our Societies, large and small, is there no egular meeting for spiritual fellowship?

Let us then seriously take to heart these things and see to it that our Church fellowship is real and deep according to our earlier traditions, whatever be the method best suited o modern conditions; and let us, because we are a Church, welcome into this fellowship lovers of Christ of *all* types in so far as they are prepared to accept our doctrine and our discipline! Years ago a Cambridge don who later became an Anglican dignitary said to me that he wished that the Church of England had such a thing as the Methodist Class-Meeting.[2] If we are not wise, we are nearing the pass when we too might wish we had it! That would be a disaster of the first magnitude, especially in view of the needs of those who are once again in civilian life after conditions of war service and of those who are being won for Christ in so many different ways. The earliest converts 'continued stedfastly in the Apostles' teaching and fellowship, in the breaking of bread and the prayers' (Acts ii. 42). That is our example from the Primitive Church.

[1] *Report of the Special Committee appointed to consider the Conditions of Membership in the Methodist Church and adopted by the Conference of* 1938.

[2] Cp. Dr. Dale, in his sermon on *The Evangelical Revival* (1879): 'The Class-Meeting is, perhaps, the most striking and original of all the fruits of the Revival, and the Methodist people should take good heed how they treat so precious and wonderful a growth. . . . I covet the Class-Meeting.'

(2) It is impossible to attempt anything approaching complete survey of the responsibilities of Methodist fellow ship without alluding to the need for statesmanship of th highest order respecting the three main constituents c Reunited Methodism. Union has taken place in our orga ization as a Church; local Circuits and Churches were encou aged to pursue the same up and down the country, and thi they have been thankful to do in very many instances. Y how much remains to be accomplished!

In this connexion I venture to quote some sentences fror the Presidential Address delivered by Dr. Harrison to th Ministerial Session of the Conference of 1945:

'The position in the Circuits is really absurd, and it i time something was done about it. I know a town o 15,000 people which has five Methodist Circuits. I heard o a little country town in East Anglia with three chapel which had so little to do with one another that one of ther might just as well have been a synagogue, and another mosque, and the other a Christian Scientist place. I hear of another place where there were two churches within tw hundred yards of each other and in two different Circuits— and no more than twenty people in either of them. . . . cannot see why money should be poured out to keep circuits independent when there is no reason why the should be independent. We must exercise patience, and turn to prayer that the obstacles may be removed.'

Surely we cannot, we dare not, be satisfied while this ca be said of the Methodist branch of the Body of Christ Happily, much can be said on the other side, but that is n extenuation of our existing complacencies. No one woul countenance ill-considered haste in pressing forwar Methodist union in any locality; for if the fellowship o amalgamating Circuits and Churches is to be real 'we must' in Dr. Harrison's words, 'exercise all the ingenuity and th grace we have'. Yet we are not exonerated in the sight of God if we refuse to exercise either. The evil of overlapping continues while other areas are insufficiently served; we are in peril of loving the sanctuary more than the people. Such an outlook is generally the cause of a misguided expenditure of effort and money, though Circuit amalgamation should not so often necessitate a reduction of the ministerial staff as its redistribution. Can we entirely acquit ourselves of a lack of appreciation of the needs of whole areas in which our Churches are placed—a lack of what might be called spiritual strategy? Is there not, on occasion, an unhelpful remembrance of past unfriendliness—perhaps even, in the secrecy of the heart, a reluctance to jeopardise one's own self-importance in any wider union? That is frank, but, we trust, not unworthy; for such a temptation endangers us all. And yet our difficulties are to be faced, not overrated; and in case after case many of them have disappeared after a local union has been effected when they seemed insuperable before.[1] Where there is a burning *desire*, and an insistence on what is believed to be the mind of Christ, a sure foundation is already laid; indeed, that is essential to any mutual approach. If Methodists of neighbouring Societies make an effort (if such be required) to know one another, to co-operate with one another in evangelism, and, perhaps regularly, to worship together, they will find the way paved toward any closer union which may be envisaged. The prayer of our Lord, 'that they may all be one', has been variously interpreted; yet, surely, there is no interpretation of it that cannot properly be applied to 'the People called Methodists'.

(3) Methodism as a 'Church' is taking part in a wider

[1] Thus a French ex-captain of the Battle of Verdun in the First World War: '*Il n'y a pas de situations désespérées, il y a seulement des hommes désespérés.* (There are no hopeless situations; there are only men who have grown hopeless about them).' *European Spring*, by Clare Boothe, p. 297 (Hamish Hamilton).

C

fellowship known as the Ecumenical Movement—a movement of the Spirit of God affecting universal Christendom,
the like of which has not been seen since the fifth century.
This movement took its rise at the International Missionary
Conference held at Edinburgh in 1910, followed by action
on the part of the American Episcopal Church, which
pressed for a full consideration of questions of Faith and
Order. After years of preparation, the first World Conference on Faith and Order met at Lausanne, in Switzerland, in
August 1927, when over one hundred 'Churches', or
Christian denominations, were represented. The Conference unanimously endorsed a Call to unity, then discussed
the subjects of the Gospel, the Church, the Church's Confession of Faith, the Ministry, the Sacraments, and the
Unity of Christendom. A Continuation Committee was
appointed to advance the cause of unity and to draft a
programme for a second World Conference in 1937. Mean-
while, our Church had been sharing in parallel world movements of the Church of Christ in the realms of missionary
endeavour, 'Life and Work', and the World Alliance for the
Promotion of International Friendship through the
Churches—all being expressions of the desire for agreement
and co-operation among all who owned allegiance to our
Lord Jesus Christ. The second World Conference on Faith
and Order met at Edinburgh in the year appointed (1937).
It considered four subjects: Jesus Christ and His Grace, The
Church of Christ and the Word of God, The Church of
Christ—Ministry and Sacraments, and The Church's Unity
in Life and Worship, concluding with a unanimous Affirma-
tion of united loyalty to Christ. A momentous outcome of
this whole movement was the founding in 1938 of a World
Council of Churches as a 'Fellowship of Churches which
accepts our Lord Jesus Christ as God and Saviour'. Some
of its main purposes are to facilitate common action by the
Churches, to promote co-operation in study, to call world

regional conferences on particular subjects, and to provide opportunity for united action in matters of common interest. The Methodist Conference annually appoints an Ecumenical Movement Committee for the World and British Councils of Churches, and also its ten representatives to the British Council. To this latter Council local councils of Churches are affiliated all over Great Britain and Ireland. Christian education, social responsibility, evangelism, international friendship, Faith and Order are certain of the subjects receiving regular and careful attention by the constituent Churches in an atmosphere of deepening fellowship. Thus, throughout the countries of the world, and in spite of war, the Holy Spirit has continued to lead and to strengthen this great work—a work which we believe will redound increasingly to the glory of God and the good of mankind. In the words of the General Secretary of the World Council:

'It is of tremendous significance that in these last years the article concerning the One Catholic Church has been confessed in a new and concrete way over against the heresies of racial religion and chauvinism. For we may now feel assured that the rediscovery of the "Una Sancta", which has taken place in the last thirty years, is not a passing hobby or fashion, but a truth which has re-entered into the life of the Churches.'[1]

Now, since Methodism is no sect, but a 'Church', her members should deem it a duty to survey the Christian landscape with wide sympathy and to cultivate the ecumenical mind. 'To me', once said Bishop Palmer, 'the ecumenical mind is the power to look at the Church in the same sort of way as the Church would look at itself if it was really *one* again.' This may not seem easy, at any rate to some of us.

[1] Reported in *The Church in the World* (pub. by the British Council of Churches), issue for December 1945.

We may be prone to think that Methodism is all that we require, which might be verging on the sectarian; we may still need to develop our doctrine of Methodist Churchmanship. *All* Christian Denominations need to explore more deeply the nature of the Christian Church. Let Methodists be assured that they have a contribution to make toward this—that they possess a largeness of heart and a longing to see a clearer vision of our Lord's purpose for His Church in all the earth!

CHAPTER V

THE PASTORAL OFFICE

(1) IN a book entitled *The English Church*, written by the Bishop of Chichester, occur these words:

'Every parish has its parson. . . . Unlike any other minister of religion, he has the privilege of visiting every house. Thus, because he is a Church of England parson, he has duties and obligations to the whole body of parishioners, whether or not they profess any care for religion, and whether or not they belong to any congregation.'[1]

Such is, of course, the general attitude of the clergy of the Anglican Church. It found expression again in a debate in the House of Lords on 8th June 1944 in a speech by the Earl of Selborne:

'The Church of England is in a different position to other denominations because that Church is responsible, not merely for her own congregations, but also for the great population not attached to any denomination in a way that no non-established Church can be.'

The plea is made that a minister of the Establishment has pastoral duties which a minister of another communion has not, and there is an historical basis for it in that the parochial system in England goes back to the seventh century. And no Methodist would deem it Christian to curtail the pastoral activities of any minister of Christ so long as these are exercised with Christian love and with full regard for denominational loyalties other than his own. But in this year of grace the Free Church minister has every right to

[1] Pub., William Collins, p. 35. Dr. Bell proceeds to describe the work of the parish parson in a way altogether admirable.

regard himself as equally privileged to exercise his own pastoral office wheresoever his conscience leads him. Anything short of this would suggest that he is a minister of a sect and not of a Church; whereas the statement that 'Free Church ministries are real ministries of Christ's Word and Sacraments in the Universal Church' was deliberately made by several Bishops of the Anglican Communion in 1923. The pastoral office of a Methodist minister is stressed throughout his Ordination,[1] and to that office there are no limits of human devising. That is implied by what we assert to be the full Church nature of the communion which ordains him. Is it not, therefore, incumbent on all Methodist ministers to emphasize in every way they can the shepherding which the Chief Shepherd has entrusted to them? The delightful duty of preparing the young, in heart and mind, for entrance into the communicant membership of the Church is only one of many such ways, followed, in accordance with the rule of the Conference, by the Recognition Service as the climax to this preparation.[2] And there are always a multitude of duties which can never be ruled by Standing Orders, but which are laid on the conscience of every true pastor. He will be a shepherd to his people, tending the homes where little ones have been baptized, watching the growth of his Sunday-school scholars in the knowledge and the love of Christ, and regularly ministering without discrimination to all who are in need. If only our

[1] e.g. the last question to the Ordinands, ending: 'Will you continually stir up the gift of God that is in you, by the help of the Holy Spirit, to testify the Gospel of the grace of God to *all* men?' (italics mine).

[2] In 1944 the Church Membership Committee informed the Conference 'that only 35 per cent. of Circuits report that services for the Public Recognition of new members have been held in the past year'; and, similarly, the Commission on Rural Methodism: 'We learn with dismay that Church Membership Preparation Classes are not being held regularly in more than 10 per cent. of our churches, although Conference has repeatedly declared that the giving of such instruction is our imperative duty.' A widespread regard for our rule in this connexion would yield incalculable results.

ministers were not expected to spend so much of their time on matters of secondary importance, or to be present so often at meetings where their presence is not really necessary, they could more freely devote themselves to the primary and most pressing opportunities of the pastorate. And to these there is simply no limit.

Yet, within our branch of the Church of Christ, the pastoral office has never been meant to belong to the minister alone. The lay leaders from the first were entrusted with an important share in it, and they, as leaders of the Society Classes, were to exercise it side by side with that exercised by the 'travelling preachers'. 'I positively forbid any Preacher to be a Leader', wrote Wesley (10th February 1783): 'Rather put the most insignificant person in each Class to be Leader of it.' These were wiser words than later Methodism has always realized. Moreover, the Conference has declared that it 'has made the care of the membership of the Church the fundamental responsibility of the Leaders' Meeting—yet it is precisely in this matter that many Leaders' Meetings never function at all'.[1] We sorely need to recover the sense of *lay* pastoral responsibility. Cannot we do more to bring home to our Methodist laity something of the extent to which they may function as shepherds of the flock? For no preacher, leader, or teacher among them need doubt that upon him or her the Head of the Church has laid the responsibility of caring for all who are attached to us by any ties, however slender, and even for those known to us who make no sort of religious profession.

(2) Beside the pastoral obligations of the Ministry and laity in the Circuits there are those which rest upon the Districts and are discharged particularly by their Chairmen. 'It is the duty of the Chairman of a District to exercise an oversight of the character and fidelity of the Ministers in

[1] *Minutes of Conference*, 1939, p. 417.

his District.[1] This duty of oversight covers a much wider field than matters of discipline: it is, in short, that of a Father in God to the whole District and to every Methodist within it. The Chairman is concerned with the suitable staffing of the Circuits, the oversight of young ministers on probation, the well-being of ministers' families, as well as the work of God throughout the area over which he has supervision. It is his care, by the consideration of the Superintendents, to visit the Circuits in order to encourage and advise, and to offer his experience and leadership.[2] Among an ever-increasing number of duties, official and unofficial, the above are examples drawn from the pastoral side alone; for the Chairman is Chairman, not only of the Synod, but also of the District. The title itself, somewhat uneasily and guardedly retained, does not commend itself to all Methodists as appropriate, while to non-Methodists it conveys little or nothing. It is quite devoid of any suggestion of pastoral significance.

The question as to whether Chairmen of Districts are able efficiently to discharge simultaneously all the duties which they now have and also those which devolve upon them in other capacities, especially those of Circuit Superintendent and pastor, has been the subject of considerable discussion. In general, let it be said that a *conscientious* fulfilment of everything that *ought* to be done in these two or three capacities, at one and the same time, is impossible: neither the District nor the Circuit can receive that sufficient pastoral attention which the Chairman himself desires to

[1] *Standing Order* 173.

[2] A Chairman is directed to visit each Circuit to which only one minister is appointed at least once in each year, and is authorized to visit any other Circuit in collaboration with the Superintendent or when, in special cases, the District Synod should direct. The provision that he 'must never interfere individually with any Circuit but his own' (*S.O.*, 155) was first made in 1792 and has been retained word for word ever since. If it still be required, perhaps its wording might be tempered with advantage'!

give. A solution of the problem has been found in some Districts by their request to have Chairmen without other responsibilities, who are thus able to devote the whole of their time to their office and to render undivided service to the wider areas. Where, however, no proper solution has been found, the problem persists—to the detriment of the work of God; and it can never be solved by being avoided, or by the encouragement of the idea that there is really no problem at all.[1]

(3) There remains a broader aspect of the Pastoral Office of the Church, to which reference has already been made. Since Methodism is not a sect, but a branch of the Church of Christ, she should aim at 'extending the influence of the Christian religion among all secular institutions' and throughout the everyday life of the world. Ever since the Divine Word became flesh and dwelt among us, the Christian Faith has never lacked social implications, and this is clear in the attitude of Early Methodism. Wesley approached the whole social problem from the starting point of the infinite value of every man in the sight of God and the need for his conversion, with the spiritual and ethical result of 'pure love reigning alone in the heart and life'. To him the salvation of the individual was 'the never-failing remedy for all the evils of a disordered world'.[2] With that as his basic conviction, he carried forward a social programme which was truly remarkable for the century in which he lived, and

[1] It is open to grave doubt whether the problem could be solved by the creation of smaller Districts. *One* reason why there have been Districts in our organization, operating on a level between the Circuits and the Conference, is that the mind of the Church as a whole might the more easily be ascertained, and a subdivision of the existing forty-six Districts would be most unhelpful to that end. Each District, too, must be strong enough in spiritual and material resources to be a successful working entity on that 'higher' level. Moreover, more Districts would mean more Connexional officials, with all that that would entail to Committees and to the Conference.

[2] *The Wesleyan Movement in the Industrial Revolution*, by Wellman J. Warner (Longmans, Green & Co.), p. 67.

which has received full treatment at the hands of several able writers.[1] Throughout her history, in varying degrees, Methodism has remembered her duty of proclaiming the Gospel in its application to the needs of society; and, since 1932, *Declarations* of the Conference, drafted mainly and in a statesmanlike manner by the Temperance and Social Welfare Department, have been issued from time to time concerning sundry social problems, and are illustrations of the operation of the pastoral office in this wider sense.[2] The approval of the Conference has also been given to certain Statements, such as those on the International Situation,[3] and the 1944 Education Act.[4]

And now, as Abraham Lincoln said in his Gettysburg oration, 'it is for us, the living, to be dedicated here to the unfinished work which they who fought there have thus far so nobly advanced'. We have been divinely delivered after a second world war, and now we, with all the nations, face an unfinished work—that of building anew the fabric of human relationships on a foundation of righteousness. Great opportunities confront the United Nations' Organization, and these will be worthily seized as it is actuated by a sense of international comradeship and moral responsibility.[5] It is precisely here that the influence of the whole Church of Christ on earth should unceasingly be exerted, even as it was exerted in 1940 when Roman Catholics and Protestants in England announced their joint acceptance of

[1] See Troeltsch, *ibid.*, II, p. 721.

[2] For example, The Drink Evil, The Industrial Order, The Christian Significance of Leisure, The Gambling Problem, The Christian View of Marriage and the Family.

[3] *Minutes of Conference*, 1945, pp. 182 ff.

[4] *Ibid.* 1944, pp. 196 f.

[5] 'We shall have to labour hard to establish peace on the unshakable foundations, not alone of material strength, but also of moral authority.' The King's broadcast, 15th August 1945.

the Five Peace Points of Pope Pius XII.[1] The World Council of Churches (not including the Roman Catholic Church) will be able to do great things in strengthening friendship between the peoples from among whom its representatives are drawn, and the British Churches' Council is active through its Department of International Friendship and its Committee for Reconstruction in Europe.[2] The Methodist Church, in turn, operates in this connexion on the British Churches' Council through her own representatives, who are chosen from the relevant departments of Methodism. In addition, both the Temperance and Social Welfare and the Overseas Missions Departments bring to bear Methodist influence directly on the world situation as occasion requires. In view of the importance for peace and goodwill of the closest collaboration on the part of the English-speaking peoples of the world, there is need for the Methodist Churches of America, Great Britain, Ireland, and the Dominions to keep in constant touch with each other, also for the organization of the Methodist Ecumenical Movement to maintain full activity.

With regard to national and social concerns, all the Churches in England hold to the five points in the second part of their 1940 Declaration,[3] and the British Churches' Council, through its Department of Social Responsibility, continually surveys various aspects of social life in conjunction with the Councils of Churches and of Social Services in

[1] Reparation for wrongs done, Progressive disarmament, An international judicature, Adjustment of needs and just demands, Development of responsibility according to the 'standards of the laws of God'.

[2] See the pamphlet, *The World to Be?*, issued by the Department of International Friendship, setting forth the moral foundations of an international order: consideration of the desires of peoples, freedom for religion, freedom from want and fear, the worth of the individual, etc.

[3] Abolition of extreme economic inequality, Equal opportunities for children, The safeguarding of the family, The sense of Divine vocation to be restored to daily work, A considerate use of God's gifts of the earth's resources.

the localities. The hold which intoxicating drink and gambling are gaining upon so large a portion of the population is unceasingly before our Temperance and Social Welfare Department, together with such interdenominational bodies as the Temperance Council of the Christian Churches[1] and the Churches' Committee on Gambling. The nation needs houses, but it also needs homes; and the attention of our own Church to this may find illustration from different angles in the work of the Methodist Women's Fellowship and in that of the Standing Commission for the Development of Methodism in New Housing Estates. Along with other Denominations, we are taking a practical interest in the very real requirement of homes for the aged. How best to serve and to challenge youth is yet another pastoral responsibility which the Churches are endeavouring to discharge both singly and together.

We thankfully acknowledge that an opportunity now exists of a very close bond between religion and education, with religious teaching given in the schools by persons of ability and Christian conviction, and in the atmosphere of worship. The need still remains, however, to train children and young people in churchmanship, and it would surely be optimistic to imagine that all the children of every family with Methodist connexions (unless attached to another Denomination) receive regular instruction in Methodist churches or Sunday schools. It might be a helpful measure to have outlined in the day schools the contribution made by the various branches of the Christian Church to the life of the nation and of the world; while occasional withdrawals to churches for worship might have value in accustoming children to enter places of worship connected with their

---

[1] Note its *Seven Point Programme for the Times*, re Youth, The B.B.C., A national licensing commission, Social centres, The waste of foodstuffs, Clubs, and Overseas responsibilities. This last point is watched by a Joint Committee of the Methodist Temperance and Overseas Missions Departments.

own homes who otherwise might hardly ever do so. The ideal solution is difficult to reach, and more so in some places than in others. But it is at least worthy of consideration that, without linking all our children with our Church and training them for active churchmanship, their undenominational instruction in 'the great simplicities of the Christian religion' might tend to lack consolidation and even to become rather a faint memory.

Hence, what has been termed the broader aspect of the pastoral office is 'exceeding broad': to quote the verse (Psalm xix. 96) in Moffatt's translation:

> '*I see a limit to all things,*
> *But Thy law has a mighty range.*'

The influence of the Church of Christ needs to be brought to bear simultaneously both on international and social problems because they affect one another. As in the preamble to the 1940 Declaration of the Churches: 'No permanent peace is possible unless the principles of the Christian religion are made the foundation of national policy and of all social life.' Much more is needed for a world in desperate straits than a little Christian flavour added on occasion to counsels of worldly wisdom. It is the Gospel which is everywhere supremely needed—the Gospel fearlessly lived and honestly and lovingly applied. For the new Jerusalem, welcomed among men, must descend out of heaven from God.

CHAPTER VI

WORSHIP

(1) THE deepening of the sense of intimate relationship between worshippers and God should always be a concern of the Church. Worship is first and foremost the adoration of God and the deliberate offering of ourselves to Him, the awareness of His glory and the condescension of His grace.

> 'Lo, God is here! Let us adore,
> And own how dreadful is this place!
> Let all within us feel His power,
> And silent bow before His face;
> Who know His power, His grace who prove,
> Serve Him with awe, with reverence love.'

That verse from a German mystic, translated by John Wesley, expresses this approach. To what extent is it the approach of Methodist worshippers? And, as a Church, do we always aim in public worship at offering our best to God? Are we not sometimes content with a bald and slip-shod service, as though, so long as worship may be 'hearty', there is no compelling need for careful thought as to its conduct? Is there not, on occasion, a tendency to tolerate musical elaborations (not all of a high order), to which the congregation is expected to listen, instead of taking pains to raise the standard of the people's worship as a whole? Are we careful to avoid either the intrusion of entertainment or the danger of anti-climax—for these are serious considerations very closely affecting spiritual impressiveness?

Church music should be an expression of worship. It is itself an offering to God, it is also a powerful instrument of uplift to the congregation; and both of these considerations should never be forgotten. The late Archbishop Lang once said: 'No sermon can have the power of uplifting hearts and minds as true and noble music can. Great music always transcends words.' And while there are many Methodist sanctuaries wherein the music could never be called 'great', in all of them it may be spiritually impressive, and in some of them it could be improved—with the co-operation of all who lead and join in the praise.[1] As far as possible, every part of public worship should be thought out beforehand: what is called 'the inspiration of the moment' is not always inspiring—when it is due to the laziness of persons with little sense of sacred responsibility.

Hymn-singing was a feature of the Evangelical Revival of the eighteenth century under the leadership of Charles Wesley, and it was no feature of any other movement until the Oxford, or Anglo-Catholic, Movement of the nineteenth made it a feature of its own. Both these movements have greatly enriched the song of the Universal Church, and now the Methodist Hymn Book of 1933 has an historical range of hymns and music far wider and more 'Catholic' than any previous Methodist publication.[2] In many of our churches this range is little appreciated; musically, the congregations still pursue the accustomed track and take but a tiny glimpse at the wonderful landscape spread before them. Our congregational singing can be as inspiring as ever, and more so, as other songs of Christendom are wisely taught and keenly learned. Among these 'other songs' are the Canticles and Psalms, which in a large number of our places of worship are not even attempted, but which would prove a helpful

---

[1] In this connexion the work of the Methodist Church Music Society is most valuable.

[2] It contains hymns which stretch through the centuries back to the Early Church, also more than 300 tunes composed during the eighteenth century and earlier. At the same time the book is truly 'Methodist': forty-nine tunes which were cast out of the 1876 book in 1904 are now restored, and twenty out of the forty-four of the 'Foundery' collection of hymns are inserted.

and truly welcome variation in our services. The singing of psalms dates from the ancient Jewish Temple and is a long tradition in church worship.[1] In our hymn-book there is a system of pointing so clearly marked as to accustom quickly any enterprising congregation in the regular singing of them. At the very least, the singing of the Canticles might take place far more frequently, especially the greatest hymn of the Early Church, *Te Deum*.[2] The quality of anthems, spiritual and technical, should be kept high as befits the worship of God, and an endeavour should be made to read to the congregation beforehand some of the words of every anthem in order that there may be an intelligent appreciation of what is being sung. It may be that, in our generally extempore manner of conducting worship, too much is made to depend on the present mood or spiritual tone of the preacher, and that too little opportunity is afforded to the congregation to take an audible and responsive part. A useful manual of responsive Orders of Worship, entitled *Divine Worship*, approved by the Conference for optional use in our churches, was issued in 1935, and could be used with profit. Even so, the second Order in the manual, which is the Anglican form of Morning Prayer, is definitely superior to the others; and this may serve to remind us of the rich liturgical tradition of Christian Prayer upon which

[1] 'Hymn-writers may rise to great heights or sink to considerable depths; the canonical writers stand alone.' *Religion in the Victorian Era*, L. E. Elliott-Binns, p. 374 (Lutterworth Press).

[2] The original hymn consisted of the first two parts only; the first part was possibly based on a third-century hymn; the second part dates from the fourth century. The third part consists mostly of quotations from the Psalms, used as versicles and responses, and was added for liturgical use in the sixth century: it is centred rather on human need than on the praise of God, and could well be omitted. See *Church Music in History and Practice*, by Winfred Douglas, Mus.Doc. (Charles Scribner's Sons, 1937), pp. 158 ff. For our congregational singing of *Te Deum* a setting to suitable chant tunes is greatly superior to, and would be a considerable relief from, the well-worn setting by Jackson.

all the Churches may draw when they will.[1] At the same time, Methodists also have a tradition of extempore prayer which they must not lose. So did Dr. Harrison express himself from the Chair to the Ministerial Session of the Conference in 1945: 'Our devotional life is very thin. It seems, almost, sometimes, as if we had forgotten the gift of extemporary prayer. We must have a richer worship.' Doubtless we still possess that 'gift'; yet our extemporary utterances are far more likely to be edifying if we give thought to their outline beforehand. Times of silent, and guided, prayer may profitably find room in our worship more than they do; also times of silence in which we listen for the Divine word to ourselves. Meetings especially for prayer have languished among us, undoubtedly to our loss. But, whether we are led in prayer extemporaneously or by set form, the complete absence of audible response in so many of our congregations (unless sung) is most regrettable.

> *'Blessed be the Lord, the God of Israel,*
> *From everlasting even to everlasting.*
> And let all the people say, AMEN.'[2]

A mark of our Churchmanship should be the reading of Lessons from both Old and New Testaments during public worship, with the aid of a lectionary; for these are times in which very many in our congregations do not read the Bible for themselves. Another mark of it is the observance of the great festivals of the Christian Year, from Advent to Trinity Sunday, which is happily so prevalent among us. Dr. Bett has observed that, while many of the hymns of early Methodism have been used by all the Churches, 'that is especially true of the hymns for the great festivals of the

---

[1] I have, of course, taken for granted the use of our *Book of Offices*, which bears a real kinship to the Book of Common Prayer.

[2] Psalm cvi. 48.

D

Christian Year'; and he points out that 'it was not the Oxford Movement but the Evangelical Revival that gave these great hymns of praise for the festivals of the Church to the English language'.[1]

(2) Sanctified culture is certainly receiving more attention among Methodists, as the example of our modern ministerial training will show. The appreciation of beauty has not always been strong among us in regard either to our buildings or their furnishings. Victorian Methodism did not give very serious thought to architectural beauty, though there *was* improvement in this regard as the nineteenth century advanced. Our chapels of those days were designed pre-eminently for preaching, and many of them could not lay claim to any particular style at all! Hugh Price Hughes, when leader of the earlier Forward Movement in Wesleyan Methodism, asserted that the Methodist Church had suffered from the fact that John Wesley had had no adequate sense of the beautiful. These words of his follow in his *Life*:

'It is high time that those of us who represent the glorious Puritan tradition should remember that there is such a thing as the "holiness of beauty" as well as "the beauty of holiness". . . . We must approach the True through the Beautiful, as well as the Beautiful through the True.'[2]

The devotional life of our Methodist youth has been greatly enriched in more recent years in school and college chapels, but that very fact may add to our problems unless we show an imaginative appreciation of the aids to devotion with which they are now provided. In such places they find spiritual helpfulness in lovely things; in Hughes' words, they can 'approach the True through the Beautiful': and so

[1] *The Spirit of Methodism* (Fernley-Hartley Lecture for 1937), p. 186.

[2] *The Life of Hugh Price Hughes*, by his Daughter (Hodder and Stoughton), p. 406.

often all this is in violent contrast to the ugliness (not just simplicity) of many of our sanctuaries which they are expected to attend at home. This is no appeal for ritual as ordinarily understood, nor is it in any sense a criticism of the plainness of chapels which have been built out of the poverty of our people and lovingly tended by them: it is simply an assertion that the appeal of the beautiful in the realm of worship is far more important than Methodists often realize. Under the influence of the Divine Spirit such an appeal is essentially evangelistic.[1]

(3) The fact of our Churchmanship makes it our duty to consider, within our natural limits, how best we may help the worship of varied types of persons who attend our sanctuaries. If we were a sect, we would assume that all the members of our congregations were of one and the same type in each locality. As we are a 'Church', it is our duty to make provision for Methodists of all types, so that (to quote once more) *every* lover of Christ' may 'find in her a congenial spiritual home'. For instance, many who enter our churches and chapels may prefer to kneel when they pray;

---

[1] In an attractive, illustrated publication, *The Planning and Designing of a Methodist Church*, by Joseph Crouch, F.R.I.B.A. (1930, Silk and Terry, Birmingham), these words occur: 'Methodism of all the Nonconformist bodies, has departed least from the practices of the Protestant Church of England, and there can be nothing incongruous in its members taking as models the buildings of the Church from which they sprang. I am of opinion that it is on the lines of the ancient Gothic style that the Methodist churches of today should be designed, but modified in such a way as to meet the special requirements of congregational worship.' Another style, a perfectly beautiful copy of pure Norman, may be found at South Anston, in the Worksop (Wesley) Circuit. It may be added that J. L. Pearson, the architect of Truro Cathedral, once remarked with regard to his design for it: 'My business is to think what will bring people soonest to their knees' (L. E. Elliott-Binns, *ibid.*, p. 354). Closely related to all this is the importance of keeping our churches clean and of avoiding ugly collections of 'junk' in what may *appear* to be unseen corners. Due regard should be shown for the Lord's Table on all occasions—including Sunday School anniversaries. The symbol of the Christian Faith—a *plain* cross—could most appropriately stand upon it.

they may feel that, for them, kneeling is the most reverent attitude; also that it assists devotion. But, in a large number of these buildings, kneeling is a physical impossibility; either the pews are too close together, or there are no kneeling hassocks, or both![1] Evidently those who were responsible for making such arrangements were accustomed to sit at prayer, and it never dawned upon them that any Methodists might wish to do anything else! Even so, provision for kneeling could be made here and there without much difficulty if the local authorities could be induced to take the broader view, and be considerate enough to act upon it. This is not necessarily a matter of reverence, for reverence is primarily an attitude of the spirit: it is simply a matter of that hospitality which we, as a branch of the Holy Catholic Church, should extend to all the varied folk who enter our portals.

Reverence, as a distinct subject, cannot, however, be absent from our thought in connexion with worship. Newman once observed: 'Nonconformists have learned to be familiar and free with sacred things as it were on principle.' Admittedly, the danger of formalism in worship may be equally great; yet it may well have been that Methodism, in common with other Nonconformist communions, merited something of that satire. To what extent do Methodists still merit it? Do we always feel, as also when arriving and departing, 'This is none other but the house of God, and this is the gate of heaven?' That is, at any rate, just what each of our sanctuaries is, whatever be its size or form; and we need to possess everywhere an attitude which links together friendliness, fervid evangelism, and the deepest reverence, as befitting men who gather in the Holy

[1] In the course of the Communion Service I have often changed the wording of the exhortation, 'make your humble confession to Almighty God, meekly kneeling upon your knees', because, while the people were prepared to do the first, they literally could not do the second.

Presence.[1] A more worshipful receiving of the offerings is symptomatic of this same attitude, as is a growing custom of remaining for a few moments in silent prayer after the Benediction until the organ begins very softly to indicate the dismissal.[2] 'Atmosphere' makes all the difference in public worship; it can easily be felt—one way or the other.

Finally, let us take thought concerning a further way in which we could minister to the people—namely, by keeping our churches and chapels open for them to be used for prayer and meditation. A closed Anglican church is an exception; indeed, if an Anglican church were found closed there would soon be an inquiry as to why it was. The theory behind this is that Anglican churches are meant for *all* the people; all may use them whenever they wish. A closed Methodist church, on the other hand, is the rule, not an exception; yet should not Methodist churches be equally meant for *all* the people? Admittedly there are risks in keeping churches open, especially in abnormal times; nevertheless, when supervision is not readily available, valuable articles could be temporarily removed and, at least, covered by insurance. Of course, we have our many activities in

---

[1] Speaking of irreverence, Dr. Elliott-Binns asserts that it is sometimes 'due to defective theology. God is reduced to such human proportions that all sense of awe is lost; and this reducing of God to human proportions comes from an unorthodox idea of the Incarnation' (*Religion in the Victorian Era*, p. 364).

[2] Frequently one has heard an organist bursting upon the congregation with *full* organ *immediately* the last syllable of the Benediction has been pronounced. It is an appalling indiscretion, and shows a complete lack of spiritual imagination. . . . Wesley in his *Journal*, under 29th March (Good Friday) 1782, alludes thus to a largely attended Sacramental Service: 'While we were administering, I heard a low, soft, solemn sound, just like that of an Aeolian harp. It continued five or six minutes, and so affected many that they could not refrain from tears. It then gradually died away. Strange that no other organist (that I know) should think of this.' (The notes in the Standard Edition of the *Journal* give the information that this organist was the father of Dr. Bunting's wife. Many modern organists now follow his example.)

schoolrooms and vestries; also there is the obvious truth that it is possible to pray anywhere. But all these considerations apply also to the Established Church, which, in spite of them, insists on keeping her doors open; and, in the realm of Christian ministration, the fact that one denomination is 'established' and another is not should make no difference. Surely our bodies of trustees throughout the land are impressed with the importance of ministering to the people at large just as are the Anglican authorities: then will they not review this situation afresh and reverse our general custom? For Methodism is no sect; she is a Church of Christ. By her open sanctuaries she would proclaim it.

CHAPTER VII

EVANGELISM

(1) WE know that the vast majority of the people of this country never 'go to Church'; it is therefore our duty, as a Church of Christ, to go to those who will not come to us. The Church is missionary by nature, whether at home or overseas: if she be not missionary, she cannot be a Church according to New Testament standards. In his sermon on *The Catholic Spirit*, Wesley defines 'a man of a truly catholic spirit' as one whose 'heart is enlarged toward all mankind'. This outlook he gave to the Methodists, and it has remained a mark of our tradition.

Evangelism must rest on convictions, so that it is vital that we should be certain of the spiritual essentials which we proclaim to the mass of the people. Human need is everywhere—individually, nationally, internationally; which only shows how deeply the soul requires what it cannot provide within itself, and 'how vain are all science, philosophy, politics, and sociology combined, to secure peace and goodwill amongst men. . . . But this is exactly what the Gospel of Christ *would* do if only it were rightly understood and faithfully obeyed'.[1] Never was there a greater incentive to earnest Christian preaching on the part of those who are prepared to think hard concerning what they preach, and who experience the power which comes with full consecration to God. Thus St. Paul: 'I maul and master my body, in case, after preaching to other people, I am disqualified myself.' And what is preached should be, centrally,

[1] Dr. Frank Ballard, *Christian Findings After Fifty Years* (Epworth Press, 1927), p. 215. This same emphasis upon the fundamental need of the Gospel for every man lies behind the Lutheran conception of 'the Sacrament of the Word', whereby the living Word, which is Christ, is, through preaching, offered to the congregation.

the Good News of the Grace of God, made known in His
Son, and made effective by the Holy Spirit. The Gospel
should be the core of every pulpit deliverance.[1] At the
same time, in the emphasis on experience there should be no
neglect of the mind, no avoidance of intellectual effort. It is
of interest to note that in his famous sermon on *The Evangelical Revival*, preached in Carr's Lane Chapel, Birmingham,
in 1879, Dr. Dale expressed his anxiety as to 'whether the
heirs of the Evangelical Revival have any earnest desire for
the gift' of intellectual inquiry in the realm of theology.
'The Evangelical movement', he said, 'has been more eager
to seek and to save the lost than to investigate the foundations of Christian doctrine; it has displayed heroic vigour
and zeal in evangelizing the world, but it has shown less
courage in confronting those great questions of Christian
philosophy, which in all the most energetic ages of Christendom have tasked the noblest intellectual powers of the
Church.' Dale returned to the charge in his Preface, written
before that particular volume of sermons was published in
1880.[2] Evidently he hit the target, for in some *Reminiscences*
of his Dr. Scott Lidgett notes that 'Dr. Dallinger's Fernley
Lecture was held up in 1880 because he advocated the
hypothesis of Evolution'.[3] We have travelled a considerable distance since then, yet there still remains a needful
reminder that, while no one can be saved by any form of
scientific knowledge as ordinarily understood, 'the mere flow
of pious platitudes in channels of ancient phraseology, with
the reiteration of hackneyed terms, is worse than useless for

[1] Methodist preachers are accustomed to a request fixed inside our pulpits
which reads: 'Please remember the children.' One which might read, 'Sir,
we would see Jesus', would be more to the point, both for children and
adults.

[2] *The Evangelical Revival and Other Sermons*, by R. W. Dale (Hodder and
Stoughton).

[3] *The Methodist Magazine*, February 1927.

ntelligent audiences'.[1] This is all the more important because of the increasing number of young people who are receiving a scientific training, and who may easily be induced to take up at least an agnostic attitude toward the verities of religion. The present plea is not for attempts at 'scientific' sermons; it is for the complete consecration both of mind and heart in the service of Christ and the evangelizing of the present age. No experience of Divine Grace can be too deep, nor can thought regarding intellectual problems be too deep, for the modern task of the Church. And, in this connexion, let us bear in mind the question of the relationship of evangelism to society and various problems which arise out of it. There is no doubt but that the Church should concern herself with the purifying of society, the championship of the down-trodden, and the help of the under-privileged. Here, again, enters the Gospel at the very centre; for Christ came to be the great Deliverer from selfishness and to rule human life on all sides of it.[2] Wesley in his evangelism aimed at saving men in body and mind as well as in spirit, and his outlook is all the more needed in times such as ours when so many thousands of our younger generation have been flung into a world upheaval amid strange circumstances and new temptations. Those who love God must love Him, as said our Lord, with all the mind as well as with all the heart; and, if we 'mean business', we shall find that we shall also have to serve Him with both.

(2) The evangelizing work of the Spirit of God by means of such departments of Methodism as Overseas and Home Missions is a constant cause for thanksgiving, and latterly we have rejoiced in a new Forward Movement in which 'Christian Commando teams' have 'offered Christ' to young

[1] Ballard, *ibid.*, p. 206.

[2] A valuable statement on this and other related subjects may be read in *Evangelism and the New Order*, being the Moderatorial Address of Dr. Newton Flew to the Free Church Federal Council on 10th April 1945.

and old—in schools, universities, factories, cinemas
wherever they have worked or gathered.[1] The campaigning
spirit of the Church must be incessant; our Lord has com-
missioned His followers in every age to 'make disciples'
and this should ever be remembered by Methodists, whose
history is essentially evangelistic. The thrill of going forth
with a team in Christ's name is an unforgettable privilege
whatever be the audience; and it has been a common
experience that the taking of one's stand for Christ amid
somewhat unaccustomed surroundings has reinvigorated
one's own faith. The insistence, however, on the need of
following up an evangelistic effort is extremely wise, and is
notable in Wesley's own case: 'I determine, by the grace of
God, not to strike one stroke in any place where I cannot
follow the blow.'[2] The following of the blow may not
result in many members being added to the Church, yet it
cannot but do untold good in establishing contacts and in
providing helpful Christian friendship. Naturally, there are
close affinities between this movement and that for the
'Rebuilding of Methodism', which has both spiritual and
material objects. When opportunities present themselves,
some of our churches and chapels will need to change their
surroundings; we shall need bravely to cut through senti-
ment, however praiseworthy, and move our causes in
pursuit of the shifting populations.

If co-operation in evangelism with other communions
can be secured, all the better; indeed, the task confronting
the whole Church of Christ is so tremendous that it is far
too vast for any one denomination. This consideration was
in Wesley's mind:

[1] An excellent description of this method of evangelism from various
points of view is available in *These Christian Commando Campaigns*, edited by
Colin A. Roberts. The term to 'offer Christ' was employed by Wesley early
in his evangelical career; see the *Journal* under dates 10th April and 17th July
1739.
[2] *Journal*, 13th March 1743.

'I met several serious clergymen. I have long desired that
there might be an open, avowed union between all who
preach those fundamental truths, original sin, and justification by faith, producing inward and outward holiness; but
all my endeavours have been hitherto ineffectual. God's
time is not fully come.'[1]

It has yet not *fully* come—if by that we mean organic union.
But it *has* come to a remarkable extent in respect of co-
working in evangelism. In the words of Bishop Hensley
Henson: 'The set of the spiritual tide throughout Christendom, and most apparently throughout the English-speaking
part of it, is toward Christian fellowship and co-operation.'[2]
This clearly underlay the 'Appeal to all Christian People' of
the 1920 Lambeth Conference. On this subject the Edinburgh Conference on Faith and Order was explicit:

'We believe that every sincere attempt to co-operate in
the concerns of the Kingdom of God draws the severed
communions together in mutual understanding and goodwill. We call upon our fellow Christians of all communions
to practise such co-operation.'

This is the very thing that the British Council of Churches
is doing, also the local Councils of Churches affiliated to it.[3]
With all such co-operation the Methodist Conference and

---

[1] *Journal*, 12th March 1764.

[2] *The Church of England* (Cambridge University Press), p. 255. Also Dr.
Flew, *ibid*.

[3] 'The British Council of Churches . . . existed to tell people in an age
when atheism was rampant that there were certain common convictions
shared by Christians of all kinds, and which had certain effects on the kind of
social life that the people led. It was the simple fact that the people of this
country were prepared to listen to the Christian Churches when they spoke
unitedly, whereas they would not listen to them in separation, still less in
antagonism.' The Archbishop of Canterbury (Dr. Fisher) to the Church
Assembly, 20th June 1945 (from *The Times* report).

the Home Mission Department are in complete sympathy.[1]
We welcome every opportunity of speaking together of the
great possession of Christian truth which we hold in
common. It is for the rank and file of all the Churches
represented on the British (or any other similar) Council
to be filled with enthusiasm for this united action, and this
they will be as they gain fuller knowledge of Christ and of
each other.

(3) Such campaigns as we have been considering contain
a lesson for Methodists everywhere, in that they should be
a stimulus to local adventure rather than a substitute for it.
How many of our Societies have never really launched an
attack in Christ's name upon their immediate neighbourhood; or, if they once did, have almost forgotten all about
it? The leadership of the ministry in District and Circuit is
vital; yet evangelism is a task for people as well as pastors.
'We set apart people in the Church, not to exercise the sole
function of mediators between Christ and His people, but
to represent in the Church the fact that every Christian has
the responsibility of leading men to Christ, and presenting
Christ to men.'[2] This is precisely what is involved by the
doctrine of the Priesthood of All Believers; and who can
tell the joy which comes when Christ has used one to bring
another to Himself! Such a responsibility in each local
Church rests in large measure upon the local court, with
Methodists the Leaders' Meeting, which is both a pastoral
assembly and a council of war. It should be the concern of

---

[1] 'In the Christian Commando Campaigns co-operation (has been) sought
and frequently experienced. It has been proved that *together* we can find
entry into firms and factories, schools and colleges, etc., denied to separate
denominations.' Home Mission Report to the Methodist Conference, 1945
(*Agenda*, p. 89). Acknowledgment should be made of the facilities for
co-operation in the spread of the Gospel afforded by the British Broadcasting
Corporation, which is doing a great work in this regard.

[2] Archbishop Temple, in an address on 'Thoughts on Reunion' (reprinted
from the *Church of Ireland Gazette*), 1935.

this Meeting, not only that the internal affairs of the Church are efficiently and happily conducted, but also that the people of the neighbourhood are evangelized. This is not simply a matter of an occasional special campaign; it should be one of a perpetual attitude on the part of the Church. A Church which sets first things first will not lack in maintaining constant contacts with the families who live around it.[1] And house-to-house visitation on this scale cannot be done by the minister alone; it must be organized and carried through by the Church members as a deliberate expression of the evangelistic duty of the Church. Open-air services may be here and there undertaken most effectively, particularly if those who speak know 'the technique'; for some of the older methods in this connexion are not now impressive. One factor, at least, is imperative—namely, utter sincerity— not alone in the open-air, but also in dealing with youth (within or without the Church), working men, or any others with whom we are endeavouring to make contact. Also, if a local Church is 'filled with the Spirit', it will overflow in an earnest *desire* to welcome 'outsiders' inside, and, with this in mind, it may consider the advisability of declaring all its pews free and unappropriated. It may, moreover, be deemed well worth the exertion to provide, especially in town and city centres, suitable social occasions in the evenings —particularly on Sundays and where cinemas are closed— at which young folk may gather, instead of perambulating the streets or frequenting public-houses. We have been too ready with our condemnations without being actively constructive. The local Church which is united in Christ, empowered by prayer, and instinct with missionary enthusiasm for those who are nigh as well as for those who are afar off, will be mightily used by the Holy Spirit for the

---

[1] 'Though a man preach like an angel, he will neither collect, nor preserve a Society which is collected, without visiting them from house to house.' Wesley's *Journal*, 29th December 1758.

uplift of the whole area in which it is placed. And, by no means least, is the manner in which Christian laymen and women may witness to the Gospel in all walks of life, and 'adorn the doctrine of God our Saviour in all things'.

These are days of terrific issues, when the gravest decisions in the spiritual life of the world are being made. On this very account the Divine call to us to go *forward* is insistent. For the Church—'the Church of pardoned sinners'—is the Body of Christ, Christ the Head, the Holy Spirit the Breath, the members indispensable to each other within a oneness of love. But the Body of Christ has wounds on it, marks of the Lord Jesus branded on it. In the war against the powers of darkness for the salvation of mankind, has Methodism wounds upon it? Perhaps this is the ultimate implication of our Churchmanship.

Now unto Him that is able to do exceeding abundantly above all that we ask or think, according to the power that worketh in us, unto Him be the glory in the Church and in Christ Jesus unto all generations for ever and ever. Amen.

Printed in Great Britain by
The Camelot Press Ltd., London and Southampton